365
GARDENING TIPS

Text: Sally Schreiber
Copy Editing: APE Overath
Cover design: BOROS, Wuppertal
Cover photography (center): (c) Ellen Fischer
(C) 2000 DuMontmonte UK, London
(monte von DuMont)

ISBN 3-7701-7006-7

Printed in Slovenia

1

For a truly organic approach that protects the structure of the soil and the millions of microorganisms living in it, cultivate a garden bed only once in your life! After that, use a hand spade or hand rake to cultivate the surface before planting next season's crops or flowers. Re-digging the bed risks destroying the delicate soil structure.

Preparing the Bed

2

Double-digging

For the initial preparation of a garden bed, especially in poor or difficult soils, double-dig the earth. Remove and set aside the top layer of soil to a depth of one spade blade. Cultivate the exposed subsoil also to the depth of one blade, incorporating compost, peat (for sandy soils), or coarse sand (for heavy, clay soils). Now return the top layer, generously mixed with mature compost. Do this only in the first year you establish the bed.

3

Hardpan

If you discover a hard, impenetrable layer of compacted soil when double-digging your garden, break up the hardpan with a pickaxe, then add coarse sand to it before restoring the layers of cultivated soil.

Soil texture

The ideal soil texture is crumbly and fine. When you squeeze a slightly moist handful, it should neither clump together (too much clay), nor should it disintegrate (too much sand).

5

As a rule, never step on the prepared soil of your garden. Compaction resulting from treading on soil virtually stymies all root growth in the area beneath. Stick to your garden paths!

Do not mix high-power fertilisers, organic or chemical, into the bed before sowing or planting. Such concentrated "food" may burn the roots of delicate seedlings. The same is true for holes you dig in order to plant or transplant shrubs.

7

Spring cultivation

Do not cultivate the soil in early spring while it is still sodden from winter rains or snow; this disturbs its delicate organic structure and causes problems later in the year. Wait until the soil is fairly dry.

8

Sowing fine seeds

For successful germination of very fine seeds, invest in a bag of special germination soil to spread thinly over the top of the bed. Its fine texture is an advantage, and it reduces the danger of "damping off" (young sprouts rotting off just above the ground), caused by the microorganisms found in normal garden soil.

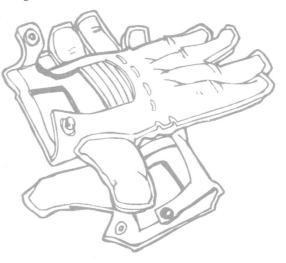

9

Raised beds

In rainy areas, try creating raised beds. Cultivate the soil, adding enough mulch, peat (for sandy soils), or coarse sand (for heavy clay soils) to form a bed 4–5 in/10–12 cm high. Make paths (at least 10–12 in/25–30 cm wide) between the raised beds by removing the topsoil from the intended paths.

10

Japanese raised garden

If you have arthritis or for some other reason can't do all the knee work gardening involves, build a Japanese raised-bed garden. From loose bricks or wood, construct a box for a bed 18-24 in/45-60 cm high. To eliminate needless bending and stretching, make it narrow enough to reach the centre easily from both sides (3-5 ft/90-150 cm).

11

Weed-free garden

For an eventually weed-free garden, try this: Early in the season, gently scratch the winter-hardened soil surface so weed seeds will germinate. Once they sprout, pull them out and sow or plant your bed. After a few seasons, the soil will be virtually weed-free.

12

In composting, layering and aeration are essential. To build your heap, alternate layers of green (garden waste and grass clippings) with woody (twigs, branches, even shredded newspapers). The woody layers supply the nitrogen needed in composting as well as air space between the more dense green materials.

Compost

13

Compost is a natural fertiliser rich in nutrients for the soil. If you cannot make your own, it can often be obtained cheaply at trash dumps.

14

The foundation

When establishing a new compost heap, first lay a foundation of several layers of thin branches. This allows air to circulate beneath the heap and may even provide a winter home for a family of hedgehogs.

If space in your garden seems too limited for composting, you can still tuck a small heap for small amounts of kitchen and garden waste in a corner, shielded by a low bush or hardy perennials.

15

For successful composting, neither too wet nor too dry is the rule. You have the right consistency if the material feels slightly moist in your hand but you cannot wring water from it.

16

When planning your garden and choosing the location of your compost heap or bin, keep in mind that extremes of either full sun or deep shade will slow down the composting process.

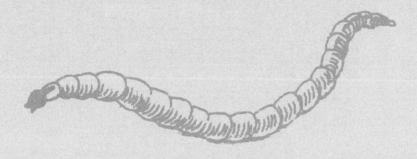

Aeration

Aerate your compost regularly—
ideally once a week. Without
oxygen, the necessary microorganisms literally suffocate,
and fermentation cannot occur.

17

18

Moisture balance

During dry periods, sprinkle your compost regularly to maintain the proper moisture balance. To keep compost from becoming waterlogged during heavy rains, throw a light tarp over the heap and weigh it down.

19

High-heat or low-heat

The microorganisms at work in a compost heap produce heat. Check to see whether you have a "high-heat" (160 °F/70 °C) or a "low-heat" (90 °F/30 °C) compost pile by checking it at the centre. A "hot" heap will be totally composted in a matter of months, whereas a "warm" one may take one to three years.

20

A cold heap

If your compost heap does not seem to be working, or even has a nasty rotten-egg odour, check its temperature. A completely cold heap indicates that the necessary fermentation is not taking place. Take the heap apart and rebuild it to get the process moving again.

21

Diseased plants

Do not add diseased plants to a low-heat compost heap—disease-causing organisms will not be destroyed and will re-infect your garden later.

22

Commercial aids

Various commercial tools can help in managing your compost heap. Garden shops offer microbial flakes that can cut composting time in half. Or to aerate a heavy heap, purchase a compost rod that easily inserts into the centre of the mound. Its pronged tip unfolds upon extraction, thus aerating the heap.

23

For evenly heated—and therefore more efficient—composting, chop or break larger pieces into a fairly uniform size before adding them to the heap.

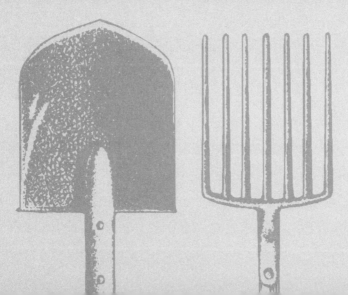

24

Lawn clippings

Let lawn clippings dry out a few days before adding them to the compost heap.
Otherwise, they tend to form dense, "thatched" layers that resist composting
and impair w: 'er and air circulation throughout the heap.

25

Space permitting, it is ideal to have two, or even three, compost heaps: a "young" pile for fresh additions, a "working" pile that you need to turn only occasionally, and a "mature" pile that is ready to use.

Beware of adding too many oak leaves to your compost heap! Their high level of tannic acid impedes fermentation.

26

Treated fruit peels

Avoid adding peels from insecticide-treated oranges, lemons, grapefruit or bananas to your compost heap. The insecticides also kill or retard the growth of healthy microbes necessary for fermentation.

28

Meat, cheese and cooked food

Do not toss meat or cheese into your compost heap—they will attract mice and other vermin. For the same reason, also limit the amount of cooked vegetables that land in the heap.

29

Mould allergies

Problems with mould allergies? Wear a light scarf or, better yet, an inexpensive painter's air filter when turning the compost heap. It's also a good idea to cover your hair, which acts as a net for the microorganisms.

30

Manure

If you have access to manure from horses, cows or fowl, regularly add a layer to your compost heap. Avoid dog or cat droppings, though, or you will draw all the neighbourhood animals to your heap!

31

Before sowing seeds, moisten them with water to promote germination. If you moisten grass seeds with a little kerosene before sowing, they won't fall prey to greedy birds.

Sowing Seeds

Dark-germinating seeds

For small, shallowly sown seeds that require dark for germination, gently water the soil first, scatter and press the seeds into the surface to the required depth, and cover lightly with an old untreated board. Check every day to see when they have started to sprout, then remove the board. Watering with an aerosol protects delicate seedlings.

33

Poppy seeds

If you've had trouble coaxing tiny poppy seeds to germinate, try sprinkling them directly onto the snow after a light, late winter snowfall—cold moisture often works wonders for poppies. They can be transplanted to their permanent locations when they are 1 in/2 cm high.

34

Light-germinating seeds

To germinate small seeds that require light, scatter them on the bed and lay a glass or acrylic sheet almost directly on the surface. Matchsticks laid horizontally work well as spacers between the soil and the plate.

35

Hard-cased seeds

To speed germination of seeds enclosed in hard casings, such as morning glories, carefully cut or file away a bit of the casing on the blunt end of the seeds and soak them in water for two or three days. Then plant the seeds 1/2 in/1 cm deep in their final garden position—morning glories do not like being transplanted.

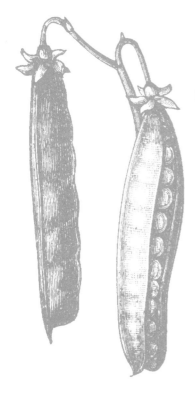

36

Beans

Some seeds, beans in parti-
cular, have little tolerance
for cold, wet soil; they
"damp off" (rot) and die.
Before sowing, make
certain not only that all
frosts are past, but that
nightly temperatures are
staying above 58 °F/13 °C.

37

Late spinach

In areas with mild winters, you can sow spinach during a warm period in late autumn. When spring begins, clear snow off the seedlings so they get enough light, but cover them with a plastic sheet if the temperature threatens to drop much below freezing (26° F/-3 °C).

38

To spread small seeds evenly, first mix them with
sand before sprinkling the mixture onto the earth.

39

Some seeds—for example, monkshood
(aconitus)—will not germinate unless they
have been frozen. If you do not want to
wait for winter to do the job for you, wrap
the seeds in plastic wrap and place them
in the freezer for two to three weeks. Then
remove and sow in pots or in the garden.

40

When transplanting seedlings, take care to get the depth right. If they are too high, too much stalk or even root is exposed, weakening the plant physically and biologically. Set too low, the stem may rot underground. With healthy seedlings, the bottom row of leaves should just clear the ground.

Seedlings

41

Indoor germination

Most seeds appreciate a fairly intense incubation experience of warmth and moisture. But once seeds have sprouted, they need a somewhat cooler temperature and plenty of light to keep from becoming leggy.

42

Greenhouse on wheels

An inexpensive plastic children's wagon can serve as a small greenhouse on wheels. Cover the bottom with planting soil, sow your seeds, and cover with a piece of glass or acrylic. (For seeds requiring darkness for germination, cover initially with a board.) Once the seeds have sprouted, depending on the temperature, wheel the wagon to more or less sunny locations, and finally to exactly the spot in the garden where you want to plant your seedlings.

43

Gentle transition

Like people, plants do not enjoy undergoing great shocks. Do not move them abruptly from a warm window-ledge or greenhouse to an exposed garden with wind and chilly night temperatures without giving the plants a few days to harden themselves to the new conditions. Place them in a cold frame and open the lid during the day, or carry the trays of seedlings outdoors to spend a few hours in the open air each day before transplanting.

Transplanting seedlings

Try to disturb the delicate young roots of seedlings as
little as possible during transplanting. Ease them
carefully from their seed trays or pots with a fork,
retaining as much of the root ball as possible. After
planting, gently but firmly pat the soil in place
around the seedlings to give the roots a hold.

45

Tools

Paint the tips of the handles of your
garden tools with bright, waterproof
paint. Doing so not only helps you find
them in the garden, it also helps remind
forgetful neighbours to whom they
should be returned.

46

Well prepared soils, rich in organic matter, do not need any additional fertiliser during the growing season. It takes several years, however, to bring soil to this point with the help of compost and slow-dissolving natural fertilisers, especially well-rotted farm manure.

Fertilisation

47

Summer nitrogen boost

Some vegetables require especially high levels of nitrogen and therefore may need a summer boost in a nitrogen-rich fertiliser. These include rhubarb, beets, potatoes, leeks, Brussels sprouts and celery, as well as many of the leafy oriental vegetables.

48

Gentle fertilisers

If you find it necessary to fertilise during the peak growing season, avoid burning the fine root hairs of your quickly growing garden plants by using fish, blood or bone meal.

49

Plant nutrients

Two of the most important plant nutrients, potassium and phosphorus, are abundant in compost and manure and dissolve only slowly in the soil. Nitrogen, in contrast, breaks down very quickly and may need replenishment in the summer by means of a chemical fertiliser if your plants seem to be suffering a deficiency.

50

Excessively leafy vegetables

Avoid feeding too much nitrogen-rich fertiliser to plants for which excessive leaf growth will interfere with the production of their vegetables. Such plants include tomatoes, cucumbers, asparagus, peas, beans, radishes, carrots, onions and garlic.

51

Green manure

You can improve your soil without a formal compost heap by planting a crop of "green manure." Alternate your vegetables every three or four years with a crop of mustard greens, clover or lupine. In late summer, dig the green manure into the soil to act as compost for the next year.

52

Natural, loose mulches approximately 5–6 in/
12–15 cm deep maintain the soil's moisture and
foster the growth of earthworms that aerate and
loosen the soil for better root growth. They also
retard the germination of weed seeds—or at least
make them easier to pull out if they do take root.

Mulching

53

Move mulch aside

After long, heavy rains rake mulch away from plants and shrubs to prevent stem rot and to allow the soil to dry out faster. In early spring, to help soil to warm faster, clear away mulch and set it aside for a little while.

54

Ward off stem rot

Plants susceptible to stem rot benefit from a light mulch of gravel just around the stems to allow good air circulation and keep moisture-retentive organic mulch away from the plant stems.

55

Bark mulch

Bark makes an ideal mulch because, unlike compost, undesirable seeds cannot germinate so quickly in it. Bark from "noble" hardwood trees is longer lasting than less expensive softwood mulches from pine and hemlock, for example, which have to be replaced every year.

56

Artificial mulches

The problems with mulches of paper, perforated plastic or artificial fleece-like material are that they provide excellent hiding places for snails and—possibly worse—keep earthworms from coming up for air during heavy rainfall.

57

When it's wet

In very wet climates or seasons, little or no mulch may be in order; removing it helps water evaporate from the soil more quickly. A scattering of gravel around plants also helps draw water more quickly from the soil.

Growing potatoes

Try this for an easy and interesting way to grow potatoes: Lay them on top of worked garden soil and cover them with 5–6 in/12–15 cm of mulch. When green shoots appear, add layers of mulch around them regularly. Keep young potatoes well covered, as excessive exposure to light activates the chlorophyll in their skin and turns them greenish.

59

Shredding mulch

If you live in a wooded area or have a very large garden, consider investing in a shredder to chop branches and other large garden refuse to fairly uniform size for compost or mulch. Some of your neighbours in a similar situation might even want to share the cost of the shredder.

60

Evening is the best time to water, particularly during warm, dry periods. This gives plants the benefit of moist soil the whole night through and into the next day.

Water and Weeding

61

Deep watering

A deep watering once a week is better for your garden than several shallow waterings. Roots are encouraged to reach more deeply into the earth for water and thus become less susceptible to drought. On the other hand, do not allow your plants to languish through truly hot periods.

62

Water the roots

When watering, direct the water as much as possible to the roots of each plant. Broad, shallow watering encourages broad shallow roots. The same is true of fertiliser; broadcasting it means most of it will simply leech away into the soil without plants benefiting from it.

Weeds

Weeds compete with flowers and vegetables for nourishment and may harbour disease as well. The most critical time for careful weeding in your garden is just after seeds have germinated, or when transplanted seedlings are still very small. The good news is that as flowers and vegetables reach full growth, they will likely shade out any weed regrowth.

64

The best way to a healthy, natural lawn is regular care. Keep it watered and fertilised, and keep it cut at a height of 1 1/2–3 in/4–8 cm to discourage excessive weed growth. Avoid chemical weedkillers, for they also destroy earthworms, friendly nematodes, and other organic life forms necessary to a healthy lawn over the long term.

Lawn Care

65

As long as you do not overdo it, treading on grassy lawns does not harm the grass and in fact spurs growth and greater density.

66

Poorly draining soil

Moss indicates an alkaline soil with poor drainage. A light treatment with lime will even out the acidity of the soil, but be careful not to allow it to soak into the root areas of acid-loving plants like rhododendrons or azaleas. Granulated limestone is the best additive; although it dissolves more slowly than the commonly available powdered lime, it poses no danger of "burning" roots even as it improves the texture of dense, poorly draining soils.

A lawn of flowers

For a bright and cheerful lawn, rake in low-growing annual and perennial flower seeds (often available as lawn-flower packets), and water well to give the germinating seeds a good start. Since some flowers, such as primroses, require winter frost to germinate, sow in both spring and fall.

68

Mowing

Do not mow your lawn too short, especially during dry periods. In the spring, especially if you have a flowered lawn, wait until the grass has established itself again after the winter and the first bloom of the lawn flowers has passed to begin mowing.

69

What is a weed

Weeds are in the eye of the beholder. Dandelions, for example, not only add colour to the lawn, but their deep roots (the source of so much frustration to formalists who wish to ban them) improve the texture of the soil, even boring through layers of hardpan to improve drainage. Their leaves are also edible and add a pleasant tang to blander greens in salads.

70

Thatch

Thatch is a layer of matted grass cuttings and densely interwoven grass roots. The compacted roots compete with each other for water and nourishment. Thatch may be the result of a hardpan layer of soil that has interfered with proper root growth, or alternatively of too rich a diet of water and fertiliser which has made the roots "lazy"–i.e., they spread out sideways to absorb the easy nourishment, rather than downwards.

71

Deep watering

During dry periods, especially in hot weather, water the lawn toward evening to a
depth of at least4–5 in/10–12 cm
To encourage deep root growth,
it is better to water less often
but thoroughly, which helps
keep grass from drying out and
discourages thatch build-up.

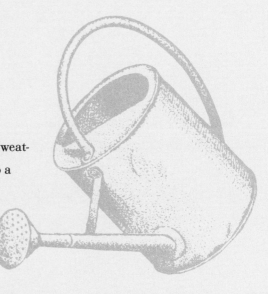

72

Grass in the shade

For shaded areas, select special shady-lawn grass seed (which you can also rake into existing grass) and mow less often to allow grass blades more time to collect the light necessary for growth.

73

Alternatives to grass

For smaller, low-use areas a low-growing, creeping variety of chamomile makes an attractive and fragrant grass substitute. Trim this "lawn" with garden shears or a rotating nylon-line trimmer.

74

Proper mowing

Wait until the lawn is dry before mowing to prevent pulling, rather than cutting, the blades of grass. Roller mowers provide the most even cut, but cylinder mowers chop the grass tips more finely. If the grass is not too long, gently rake the cuttings back into the lawn as "instant compost."

75

Autumn leaves

In the autumn, rake up fallen leaves and remove them to the compost heap. Leaves left on the lawn cut off light and cause brown spots, and they prevent proper water evaporation, leading to more potential for lawn disease.

Edging

To keep a neat, straight edge on your lawn, lay
a plank on the grass and cut along its edge
with a half-moon spade. For a curved border,
lay a hose on the ground and follow its
outline with a spade or an edger.

77

Chickweed

Another common lawn "weed" that is actually a garden friend is chickweed. The tiny seeds and delicate green leaves are a favourite of sparrows and other small seed-eating birds. If you have a parakeet, place a handful of wet (untreated!) chickweed grass occasionally in the bottom of its cage.

During the growing season, mow the lawn once a week, but not too short, so that soil does not dry out and the grass does not burn. In summer, allow grass to grow a little taller than usual.

79

Grass cuttings

In dry weather, allow grass cuttings to lie on the lawn; they will fertilise the soil as they begin to compost. If it rains, however, remove the cuttings to prevent them from rotting.

80

A large tree with a well-branched root system needs to be watered and fertilised over a broad area to nourish all the roots. A good rule of thumb is to assume that the root system extends out to the farthest reaches of the crown.

Trees

81

Grass under trees

Keep grass well mowed under the crown of a tree, for if allowed to become too lush, it competes with the tree for water and nutrients in the soil.

82

The best way to protect fruit trees from hungry birds is by covering them with a blue net. Make certain the mesh is small enough that birds cannot entangle themselves in it.

Fruit trees

83

Pest prevention

In late summer or early autumn, set aside time to bind broad strips of corrugated paper loosely around your fruit tree trunks. Leave them there for a week, then carefully remove them and burn the paper. This eliminates many harmful insects that would have liked to winter in the bark of your trees.

84

Spring trim

Remove all old or weakened wood from your trees in the spring, not only for the sake of a healthy harvest, but to avoid inviting pests that take advantage of weak or rotting branches and bark.

85

Spraying your fruit trees lightly with a mineral oil spray before buds begin to open will suffocate newly hatching plant lice and other pests.

When transplanting fruit trees, make certain that the grafting knot is 2 in/5 cm above the ground. Otherwise, undesired shoots will rise from the rootstock.

87

Fruit trees need steady moisture when they are in bloom, or they will lose most of their flowers, and with it, your potential harvest.

88

Summer watering

In the summer, just as apples and pears reach maturity,
make sure the trees' roots are deeply watered.

89

Wet feet

No fruit tree appreciates "wet feet." All fruit bearers, but especially plums and cherries, thrive best in well-drained soil.

90

Diverting birds

If your garden area is large enough, you can lure greedy birds away from your precious cherries and plums by planting chokecherry, mountain ash, or dogwood near your orchard. Birds in fact prefer sour fruits to sweet.

91

Apple trees

Apple trees are easy to care for, but they do not like windy spots. Steady wind
seriously stunts their growth.

Warmth-loving peach and apricot trees can be grown successfully in colder climates on the south side of a building.

92

93

A row of thickly planted garlic cloves around the trunk of a peach tree will help to fend off peach borers.

94

Early picking

If your cherries and berries are nearly ripe and heavy rains are threatening, pick your crop early to prevent them from becoming "water-logged" and tasteless.

Bird nets

Bird nets to throw over your
cherries and berry bushes are
a worthwhile investment. It is
entirely possible to lose almost a
whole crop within one or two days.

96

Cherry trees

In our grandparents' day, sweet cherry trees
required a variety of companions for polli-
nation. Many of the new varieties are now
self-pollinating—a real boon for
small garden areas.

Shady nut trees

Not only do walnut and chestnut trees provide nuts, they
make wonderful shade trees as well. In spite of their strong
trunks, however, they prefer a somewhat sheltered location.

98

Hazelnut hedges

Hazelnut makes a wonderful garden hedge. A hedge of hazelnut bushes around your orchard will also ensure that enough bees are present to pollinate your fruit trees.

99

Pear trees

The pear tree, unlike the apple, forms a long taproot. When transplanting, shorten it by about a third by cutting it off at an angle to encourage root growth.

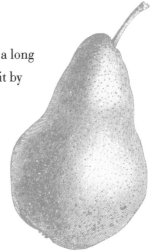

100

To give a natural look to lawns and meadows, scatter a handful of bulbs around your feet and plant them where they fall, then move on to another spot. This works well even in shady areas under deciduous trees, whose leafless branches let through the necessary sunlight.

Flowers

101

Full flowers

For fully developed flower heads, set
spring bulbs into the ground before
the first autumn frosts.

102

Fertilising bulbs

While bulbs already contain within themselves much of the energy for growth, a dosage of bonemeal will nonetheless benefit their roots. Before setting a bulb, mix a spoonful (size according to the size of the bulb) of this mild organic fertiliser into the soil at the bottom of the hole.

Moles

To prevent moles from
disrupting your lawn and eating your
bulbs, set out an inexpensive, battery-
operated thumping apparatus that taps
the surface of the earth at regular intervals with a small hammer-like weight.
Earthworms (and all creatures living
above the earth) are undisturbed, but
the sensitive moles will think a rock
band has moved in upstairs and seek
new and distant quarters.

104

Preserving bulbs

To preserve summer bulbs through the
winter, carefully dig them after their leaves
have died back, and hang them in old
nylon stockings in a cool, dark place.
Circulation of air around bulbs prevents
them from rotting.

105

Bare spots

Bare spots in your spring bulb plantings indicate time to prepare for the autumn planting. Mark the spot by placing a wooden, round-headed clothespin into the ground. If necessary, note the kind, size, and colour of the bulb you need to replace with an indelible marker on the clothespin.

106

Planting bulbs

Plant bulbs a little on the shallow side rather than too deep, for you can always mound a little more earth over tender growing tips that appear too early in the spring. Bulbs that are too deeply buried are often too weak to bloom by the time they finally reach the surface—if they reach the surface at all.

Encouraging healthy bulbs

To encourage healthy bulbs for the next season, dead-head flowers as soon as the bloom begins to fade—break off the flower before it begins to produce seed so that all the plant's energy goes to bulb growth. For the same reason, allow wilting leaves to soak up sunshine, binding taller leaves together if necessary to prevent them from falling over. Once the leaves have turned mostly brown, cut them down to the ground.

108

Forcing bulbs

You can force bulbs to bloom several weeks earlier than usual by burying them to the required depth in a pot of sandy soil mixed with a teaspoon of bonemeal. Water slightly and place the pot in a cool cellar. In later winter or early spring, bring the pot into a cool, bright room.

Planting small bulbs

To quickly plant many small bulbs (crocus, snowdrop, etc.), dig the holes by simply pushing the tines of a garden fork into the ground to the requisite distance, then enlarge the holes by moving the handle in a circular motion. Drop bulbs into place along with a little bone meal, fill the hole with soil, then close the grass on top.

110

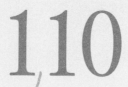

Spring treat

For a special spring treat, plant snow-drop, crocus, grape hyacinth, and low-growing daffodil and tulip bulbs randomly about your lawn in the autumn. Except for the colourful tulips, the others will become natu-ralised and bloom in subsequent years. To encourage future growth, postpone mowing in the spring until the bloom has passed and the leaves have begun to die back.

111

The flowers of both the zucchini and the nasturtium are edible in salads and take well to stuffing.

Individual Flowers

112

Anemones are an easy-to-grow bulb
reaching a height of 8–10 in/20–25 cm.
An old proverb says that the hills of heaven are
covered with anemones.

113

Anemone bulbs may be planted either
in the autumn or early spring for bloom
in the early summer.

114

Autumn crocus

For a colourful autumn lawn or garden bed,
plant a smattering of special autumn crocus
bulbs in July.

Giant allium

The giant allium is a rewarding plant for children to observe because of its quick growth and impressive size (3–3.5 ft/90–110 cm).

116

Gladiolus

Plant the bulbs of the white, star-like Abyssinian gladiolus varieties, as well as the "old fashioned" stalks, in mid-spring. Remove them after blooming, cut their stalks down to 3–4 in/8–10 cm, and store the bulbs in a cool, dry place for the following year.

Iris

Take advantage of pond edges or swampy areas in your garden by planting rhyzomatous irises (i.e., not the bulb variety) or arum lilies. Varying colours and heights of irises ranging from 6 in/15 cm to more than 3 ft/1 m make for interestingly textured landscapes.

118

Since most flowers need a good bit of sun, avoid planting flowerbeds on the north side of buildings or in the shade of other plants.

Beds & Borders

119

Garden paths

Rake grass cuttings onto your garden paths to keep them weed-free. The bottom layer will begin to compost, while the upper one keeps your feet dry.

120

Foolproof border

For a nearly foolproof flower border for the full sun, plant Shasta daisies, astilbe, rudbeckia, phlox, oriental poppies, and daylilies. Best of all, they are all perennials and will come back the following year, especially if you trim the dry stalks down to within 2–3 in/5-8 cm of the ground in the late autumn.

121

Self-sowing seeds

Many flowers that belong in a typical old-fashioned garden are self-sowing. Hollyhocks, bachelor's buttons, snapdragons and marigolds reseed and spring up again the following year—although their appearance improves with your guiding hand.

122

Perennials

When the stalks of last year's perennials begin to sprout new leaves, it is time to sprinkle a handful of natural fertiliser in a radius of several inches/5–10 cm around the plants. This encourages roots to reach outward and stabilises later flower stalks against wind and rain.

It is especially important, with flowers like marigolds, columbines, forget-me-nots and hollyhocks, to remove the blossoms before they go to seed. Otherwise they might just take over the garden!

124

Pansies, a member of the violet family, can be sown in a bed in late summer for spring bloom. In the early spring, they should be set into place as soon as the soil can be worked.

Pansies

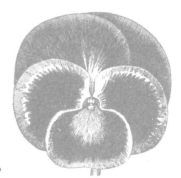

Blossoms

To extend the growing season
of pansies, pinch off the
flowers just as they pass their
peak; this deadheading encourages new growth. Also,
make certain their soil always
remains moist as the sun rises
higher in the spring. The edible
pansy blossoms make a pretty
garnish for salad plates.

126

Location

For summer bloom, sow pansy seeds in a bed in the spring. Pansies don't stand up well to heat, so set the young plants in a cool, shady location.

127

Many perennials tolerate or even prefer shady conditions: Monkshood, delphinium, columbine, Lenten rose, astilbe and foxglove are among the impressive favourites.

Flowers for Shade

128

For a shady area with acid soil, azaleas are a good bet—but keep them away from the alkaline-loving helleborus (Christmas rose)!

Members of the rhododendron family, including azalea, prefer partial shade. Their glowing foliage and deep green leaves lose none of their colour when they are moved out of full sun.

129

130

Rhododendrons over winter

When rhododendrons and azaleas die during the winter, it is usually not due to cold but because their roots have dried out. Freezing temperatures prevent their roots from getting the water that they need. The secret to overwintering is to water well before the ground freezes, and to mulch the ground beneath and around the bushes sufficiently to retain the necessary moisture.

131

Trimming flowers

Cut away lilac flowers that have turned brown for improved bloom the following year. The same is true for rhododendrons, whose dead flowers can be broken off with your fingers.

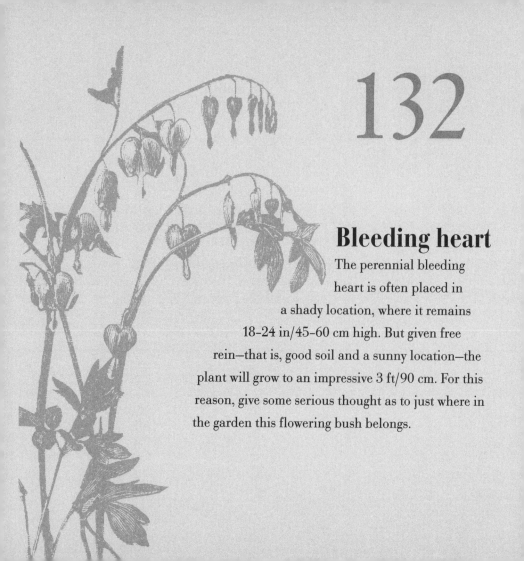

Bleeding heart

The perennial bleeding
heart is often placed in
a shady location, where it remains
18-24 in/45-60 cm high. But given free
rein—that is, good soil and a sunny location—the
plant will grow to an impressive 3 ft/90 cm. For this
reason, give some serious thought as to just where in
the garden this flowering bush belongs.

133

Propogating

Because the bleeding heart is very difficult to start from seed, look for a healthy young specimen at a garden shop, and give it several years to establish itself in your garden. Once it has really taken root, propagate with cuttings from the growing tips rooted in a mixture of peat and potting soil—for yourself, or as gifts to friends.

134

Vinca lawn

For an evergreen ground cover, especially in shady areas, plant vinca (4–5 in/ 10–12 cm) instead of grass. In late spring the "lawn" will be coloured with light purple flowers.

135

Forget-me-nots

For moist, shady areas, consider setting out a few forget-me-nots. Where conditions are right, they will increase naturally over the years.

136

Astilbe

The deep red to white waving fronds of the perennial astilbe, beautiful in sunlight, are even more impressive in their ghostly airiness in a shady nook of your garden. When choosing a colour, consider the background against which they will stand.

137

Helleborus (Christmas rose)

The Christmas rose prefers not only shade, but also an alkaline soil.

138

If your lilac bush has grown out of hand, cut it back severely after blooming. You will be rewarded by new, even fuller growth in the second year.

Impressive Flowers

139

Columbine

In terms of both colour and geometry, the biannual columbine offers a unique focal point in your garden. Plant it where the geometry of its clearly defined, looped inner petals can be admired.

140

Bachelor's buttons

Bachelor's buttons range in colour from purple to blue to pink to white, and make excellent cut flowers for the vase and for drying. If you leave them in the garden to reseed, which they gladly do, within two years you will be left, interestingly, with only the blue variety. The hybridised bachelor's buttons will revert to their parent plant, the blue cornflower.

141

Staking perennials

Some high growing, heavy-blossomed plants like delphinium, foxglove and peony will need to be staked. Bamboo sticks, 5 ft/1 1/2 m in length and driven deeply into the earth, work well and blend into the natural background.

142

Geraniums

Geraniums overwinter well in a cool and especially dry place. In spring, cut them back to the desired size and set into window boxes or the garden.

143

Geraniums are easy to propagate in autumn: Cut a growing tip with several leaves, remove two or three of the bottom leaves close to the stem, and bury the stems in a shallow pot with moist soil.

144

Geraniums make excellent balcony plants because they appreciate rather dry soil and not too much fertiliser.

145

Peonies

The glorious peony—also known as the Pentecost rose—blooms in late spring and can tolerate full sun to moderate shade.

146

Care of Peonies

Cut peony plants back almost to ground level in the autumn, and fertilise them in early spring. Such heavy development of foliage and flowers clearly requires heavy feeding.

147

Iceland poppies

The Iceland poppy, with its softly glowing colours, will bloom throughout the summer—unlike its grander Turkish cousin, which prefers cooler temperatures.

148

Turkish poppies

While the 3- to 4-foot/90–110-cm Turkish poppy blooms best in spring, it can be cut back for later, more modest bloom during the summer.

149

Taproots

Turkish poppies have very deep taproots and therefore do not take well to transplanting. Since they do not thrive in acid soils, make sure the soil around them receives a good dose of lime.

150

The sword iris (iris germanica), unlike its cousins, prefers drier soil.

151

Lupine make a good background to your garden and improve the soil by fixing nitrogen. Be aware that they do not like to be transplanted.

Campanula

Campanula's lovely blue and violet bells (also in white) are available in both tall varieties (24 in/60 cm) and dwarf sizes suitable for the rock garden. Whatever your choice, you will find them an extremely easy to care for, "thankful" flower.

153

Petunias

Petunias love humusy, fertile soil. Pinching back
the buds in early summer initially retards the
bloom but results in untold riches later.

154

Tuberous begonias

Tuberous begonias make a glowing addition to shady balconies. Just be sure to plant them with the rounded side of the tuber facing downward.

155

Alyssum

Not only do alyssum form a low, dense and easy-care border in front of taller flowers, or even as an elegant touch around your vegetable beds, but they are also a favourite of bees—which in turn will help pollinate all the other plants in your garden.

156

Low maintenance

Alyssum not only places few demands on the gardener; it is one of the few flowers that actually thrive in poor conditions. Keep fertiliser away from it, and do not overwater. You can even convince it to bloom twice if you cut back the dead flower heads in mid-summer. In 2–3 weeks, the sturdy little tufts will produce another batch of blossoms.

157

Snapdragons

Snapdragons range from dwarves to sturdy stalks of 2.5-3 ft/60-90 cm in height. They make excellent cut flowers and will continue to bloom—but on multiple stalks, weaker and shorter than with the first bloom. Their seeds, however, will sprout underneath the parent plants, and seedlings can be removed to another bed for next year's garden.

158

Delphinium

The deep blue-to-purple colour of the perennial delphinium makes a striking accent behind rose bushes, or to the side of climbing roses. Whether in the garden or in the vase, delphiniums and roses complement each other.

159

Larkspur

The annual version of the delphinium is the larkspur, which offers a greater range of colours—from purple through the blues to pink and white. Both the perennial and annual varieties make excellent, long-lasting cut flowers.

160

Snail attacks

Delphiniums tolerate shade well and enjoy moist soil. Then again, so do snails, and tender young delphinium plants are often subject to snail attacks. If you can help them survive the early danger, snails will have little interest in the tough stems of mature plants.

161

Grass carnations

The little grass carnations are not true carnations. They thrive particularly in rather poor, sandy soil, just as their Latin name, *Armeria Maritima*, suggests.

162

Carnations

The lovely clear colours of the white, pink or red carnation demand even moisture and rich, weed-free soil. But however much they add too your garden, their pungent smell makes them rather unwelcome houseguests in large numbers.

163

Children enjoy watching the growth of the tall stalks of the shade-loving lemon balsam, which also invite bees to your garden to pollinate the other plants.

For Children

Sunflowers

Sunflowers are the sentinels of the garden—some mammoth varieties reach up to 10 ft/3 m in height! Try planting a row of them as a screen for your compost heap. The speed at which they grow shows that they are heavy feeders, making proximity to the compost an ideal location for them. In autumn, harvest the heads for sunflower seeds—but leave a few standing for the birds, as well.

165

Old-fashioned garden

For an idyllic, old-fashioned garden, plant a corner of your garden with corn, interspersed with sunflowers and surrounded by a few pumpkin plants.

166

Sun followers

Even very young children are fascinated by watching quick growing sunflowers turn their heads to follow the course of the sun across the sky.

Lobelia

The jewel-like blue tones of the delicate lobelia do best in a not-too-rich soil. Cutting them back after their first bloom will inspire a second bloom.

167

Portulaca

The brilliant, jewel-like colours of the delicate portulaca do best without fertiliser.

168

169

Salvia

For a red carpet of flame in your summer garden, plant a bed of salvia.
Two years of mass plantings bring about the best effect.

170

The cheerful marigold, while easy to grow, is a true snailmagnet. Therefore, either sacrifice your marigolds or set traps to draw the snails away from your other garden plants.

Care of Flowers

171

Dahlia

Everyone knows the large and showy dahlias of the garden. But there are also dwarf varieties for flower boxes, just as rich in colour and as long blooming as their larger cousins, as long as soil is kept adequately moist.

172

Gentian

The gentian is another perennial that offers a colour range from deep blue through pink to white—and does well in shade, to boot. For the deepest, truest shades, though, give the gentian full sun.

173

Tending to asters

Asters need some tending. Taller varieties may need staking, and perennial varieties must be cut back severely in the fall to encourage new growth the next year. Otherwise, the plants become scraggly and produce poorly. The reward for proper attention, however, is not only the beauty the flowers add to your garden, but also their stamina as cut flowers.

Annual asters

Annual varieties of asters won't
thrive if planted a second season
in the same flower bed. Wait at
least three years before a second
planting.

175

The cheerful, easy-care daylily will grow even in partial shade and moist soils, although for best colour they do appreciate the sun.

176

The almost indestructible daylily forms new bulbs underground and needs to be divided every two or three years.

177

Locating cyclamen

The cyclamen, or Alpine violet, blooms in the autumn and then dies back, making it easy to overlook while renovating your garden in warmer weather. Mark the locations of the roots with a small, painted stick.

178

Fall tending

To ensure that your chrysanthemums and asters do well year after year, cut them down nearly to ground level in the autumn after blooming. Dividing the clumps after a few years is equally important. Dig up the entire root ball and carefully pull it apart into two or three sections. Discard spindly or dead roots, and replant in the desired locations.

Poisonous perennials

Some of the loveliest shade-loving perennials have highly poisonous leaves and flowers: monkshood (*Aconitus*), foxglove (*Digitalis*) and the Christmas and Lenten roses (*Helleborus*). Make certain children do not put any parts of these plants in their mouths.

180

Oleander

The beautiful oleander is highly poisonous. See to it that neither children nor cats attempt to chew on its leaves or flowers.

181

Late bloomers

The chrysanthemum is one of the most loyal
of flowers as autumn turns into winter.
Blooming in late summer, they retain
their blossoms and leaves until
the frosts become really severe.

182

Chrysanthemums

While the originally oriental chrysanthemum comes in many different sizes and colours, all need to be cut down almost to ground level in late autumn or early winter after blooming to encourage the desired full, bushy growth the following year.

183

Unhealthy chrysanthemums

Chrysanthemums are perennial and well worth the care they require—namely, staking and cutting back after blooming. They are also susceptible to rust and mould. When they sicken, it is a sign that the soil of their bed is also unhealthy, and the plants must be dug up in late autumn and transferred to a wholly new location.

184

Ivy

Coffee grounds left standing in water make an excellent fertiliser for ivy.

185

Except in areas with extremely severe climates, roses are
best planted in the autumn to allow the roots time to
settle in before spring growth.

Roses

186

Before planting

To give your new or transplanted
rose bushes a head start, soak
the roots in water for an hour
before planting them.

187

Depth

Unlike with fruit trees, the grafting knot of roses must be set 1–2 in/3–5 cm under the soil surface.

188

Spacing

Roses are heavy feeders, especially the larger specimen blooms. They also appreciate plenty of room around their roots, so do not crowd your bushes together.

189

In late autumn, mound peat
around the stems of your roses
to a height of 7–8 in/18–20 cm.

190

A dusting of sulphur in the spring
protects roses from leaf rust.

191

Pruning

It is best to prune roses neither too early nor too strongly in the autumn. Ideally, wait until spring, when you can see which stems have survived the winter.

192

Moisture

The soil around a rose must always be kept moist to a hand's depth; when they are in bloom, water them more often than usual.

193

Root growth

Especially in the spring, it is crucial that roses receive enough water and fertiliser to encourage root growth. If the soil feels dry 6 in/15 cm under the soil, soak the roots thoroughly with a garden hose. To discourage mould, avoid spraying the leaves.

194

Ladybugs

Roses heavily infested with plant lice will benefit from ladybugs. Set as many of the louse- and aphid-hungry insects as possible onto the plants.

195

Stinging nettles

Think twice before eradicating stinging nettles from your garden. These useful plants can be prepared as a vitamin-rich soup or vegetable, similar to marigolds or beets, and they are also an effective deterrent against plant lice. Soak about 2 lb/1 kg of the nettles in 10 quarts/10 litres of cold water for 24 hours, strain through a sieve, and spray affected plants.

196

Because some herbs contain essential oils that repel insects, locate your herb garden close to the kitchen window, where cooking odours tend to draw insects into the house.

Herbs

Decorative use

Some herbs serve double duty in the garden as ornamental plantings. Lavender, especially the newer, deep violet varieties, makes a beautiful border for garden steps or along paths. Hardy rosemary, with its grey-green needle-like leaves, gives texture and depth even to a winter garden. Bay can be trimmed to shape and lends itself to topiary art. The delicate, graceful anise forms a lovely background for lower growing plants in summer.

198

Chives

Chives contribute much to the garden long before they reach the salad bowl. Interplanted with lettuce and tomatoes, the pungent smell of chives wards off many insect pests. Planted in a row, chives make a beautiful border, dotted with spiky lavender flowers in the second year.

Herbal barbecue

When grilling in the garden, toss a few herbs on the hot coals. To help the herbed smoke permeate the meat or vegetables, make a loose tent of foil over the grill. Particularly favourable are basil (dried pods or leaves), marjoram, rosemary and sage (especially for chicken), and savoury. To add a delicate flavour, bind several sprigs together to use as a basting brush.

200

Herb garden

Since their roots like good drainage, herbs thrive in raised beds. Once
established, an herb garden may well remain in place over many years, even
decades, so it is worth building the walls of sturdy planking or stone.
Locate it close to the kitchen for easy access.

201

Herbs in shade

Although many herbs require a good deal of sun to develop full flavour, there are a few which tolerate partial shade and moist conditions. Among the favourites for such locations are chives, lovage, parsley, the mint family, and lemon balm (melissa).

202

In rock gardens

A few herbs that prefer dry conditions can be grown in a rock garden—or even between patio stones. The thyme family and creeping savoury do particularly well there, with the pleasant side effect of releasing their fragrance when accidentally stepped on.

203

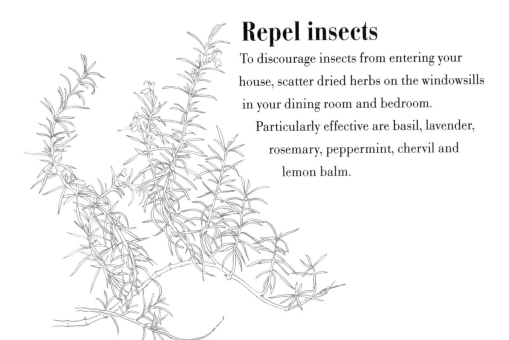

Repel insects

To discourage insects from entering your
house, scatter dried herbs on the windowsills
in your dining room and bedroom.
Particularly effective are basil, lavender,
rosemary, peppermint, chervil and
lemon balm.

204

Drying herbs

To preserve both the leaves and seeds of herbs, cut the stalks at the base, tie the heads in a small cheesecloth bag, and hang the herbs to dry in a cool, dark, well-aerated cellar.

205

Create a strawberry "farm" in your small garden plot or balcony by boring a generous series of 1-in/2.5-cm holes in the walls of an untreated barrel. Fill the barrel with rich garden soil, and set the young strawberry plants into the holes (avoiding true north, unless you are willing to turn the barrel). Keep the soil moist, but not wet. You will not have to crouch to hunt for your strawberries, and it will be easier to spy snails. To fend off hungry birds, simply throw a net over the barrel.

Berries

206

Planting strawberries

The point at which a strawberry's roots join the crown is a small and very important ring. When planting, be sure this ring lies upon the surface of the soil—too low, and the plant will die; too high and the growth will be weak and spindly at best.

207

Year-round strawberries

Year-round strawberries? It's possible with the so-called alpine varieties, available in red, yellow and white. The small berries are perennials and, unlike their larger cousins, propagate themselves by new growth at the crown rather than by runners. As the plants become denser, they need separating every few years. The low-growing bushes (8–10 in/20–25 cm) make an attractive border around flower or vegetable beds and are particularly popular with children.

Propogation

You can propagate the perennial alpine strawberries from seed. Because the tiny seeds need light to grow, scatter them in cool weather on finely prepared soil, and prevent dehydration by covering with a glass plate raised slightly on matchsticks. At this stage, avoid intense direct sunshine. When seedlings have reached the two-leaf stage, transfer them to intermediary pots.

209

Mulch for strawberries

Excelsior, often given away without charge by stonemasons, makes an excellent mulch for strawberries. It does not mat and helps keep the berries away from the wet earth.

210

Raspberry bushes do not appreciate being transplanted, so think carefully about where you want to set them—perhaps against a fence for support.

211

Cut the bearing stalks of raspberries back to the ground after the harvest. Berries form on the young, two-year-old stalks.

212

Early harvest

Cherries and berries mature very quickly once the fruits begin to form. Several days of rain just before harvest can cause a "flavour washout." If several days of rain are forecast, consider harvesting your berries a bit early rather than allowing them to become watery.

213

If you live in a dry region or have especially porous soil, set your vegetables a bit further apart than recommended to ensure that their roots do not compete for precious water. Be sure to mulch, too!

Vegetables

Garden planning

Before starting a vegetable garden, observe which way the light will strike it. Place tall-growing plants—full-size tomatoes and pole beans, for example—to the north, so as not to shade the shorter vegetables. Plant ground-covering vines, such as mallow (squash), along the edge of the garden, where their trailing vines won't cover valuable garden space.

215

Late-harvesting vegetables

Plant your various late-harvesting vegetables, such as Brussels sprouts or kale, in their own area so that you can prepare the rest of the garden for winter without disturbing these late bloomers.

216

Layout

If your vegetable garden is on a slope, run your rows perpendicular to the incline to prevent water and nutrient run-off.

217

Permanent vegetables

Some vegetables are permanent residents in your garden—asparagus, artichokes and the unrelated Jerusalem artichokes, for example. Set aside a permanent place toward the north of the garden for these tall plants so that they do not shade your more quickly growing summer vegetables.

218

Watering

Too much water makes vegetables less flavourful, especially tomatoes, peppers and carrots. Especially as the tomatoes reach maturity, cut back on the watering a day or two before harvesting.

219

Successive plantings

For quick-growing vegetables, save space in your garden for successive plantings. Sow a limited number of radish, spinach and lettuce seeds—only as much
as you can eat—every two weeks, keep them well watered, and harvest as
needed. With spinach and non-heading lettuce varieties, small families may
harvest the larger, mature leaves every few days from a series of plants, leaving
the core to develop further. Only when the lettuce threatens to bolt should you
cut the stem and bring the entire lettuce into the kitchen.

220

Many vegetables can be grown in containers if you have limited space or poor or even diseased soil. It is worth investing in good, rich potting soil for this purpose. If you do use soil from your own garden, sterilise it in your microwave, in small batches. To ensure that rays pass through the soil mass, moisten the soil slightly.

Container Planting

221

Preparation

Container vegetables need adequate nutrition and water from the beginning and throughout their lives; roots cannot reach beyond a container to find what they need. Adequate drainage is equally important. This means one or more drainage holes of 1/2 in/1 cm, covered with a stone or bit of broken pottery to keep the soil from washing out too fast.

Wind protection

Although container vegetables dry out more easily than their garden cousins, wind is just as serious a threat for both of them as direct sun. On particularly windy days, move containers to a bright but protected spot. If this is impossible, water as necessary during the day.

223

Fast-growing vegetables

Fast-growing vegetables with short- to medium-length roots—lettuce and radishes, for example—are usually the best choice for containers. Summer vegetables such as tomatoes (shorter varieties) and peppers also do well. They appreciate the warmth gathered by the walls of the containers, as long as they are kept well watered and fed.

224

Rules for success

Two rules of thumb for success in container gardens: Choose as large a container as your space allows, and cover the bottom of the container with a layer of pebbles at least 1/2–1 in/1–2 cm deep (depending on the size of the container) to keep the plant from becoming root-bound at the bottom.

225

Working the soil

Container vegetables must be well watered, but this leads to soil compaction. Have extra potting soil on hand to top off your container as the soil level sinks, and mix the soil with coarse sand or peat to work against the compaction.

226

Cool-weather crops

Slower growing cool-weather crops, such as members of the cabbage/broccoli family, do not usually do well in containers because of the inevitable heat build-up. Save container space for more grateful, quicker growing vegetables.

227

Salad greens

For lettuce and other quick-growing salad greens, enrich the soil
immediately around the roots with
a natural fertiliser just as the
young plants begin their growth
and several times thereafter.

228

When watering lettuce, water gently around the stem and even under the leaves. Avoid pouring water directly into the heads—it makes them less compact. If the day is hot, water the soil—not the leaves!—again in the afternoon.

Lettuce

Salad garden

To sow an easy-care salad garden of lettuce, field greens and even kale, draw a shallow "path" through the soil (about 2 in/5 cm wide), and scatter your seeds a bit more thickly than normal. You will end up with a densely packed row, but cull only as needed, just when you need a few young leaves for a salad. From the remaining plants, harvest only the outer leaves.

230

Sun and water

While lettuce needs sunlight for quick growth, it also loves to keep its feet wet. A bit of light shade in the heat of the afternoon, provided by taller neighbouring plants, will keep lettuce from bolting too quickly.

231

Fertiliser

Chicken manure makes an excellent fertiliser for lettuce. Spread it around the roots of the plants, and avoid getting it on the leaves for easier washing later.

232

The sturdy and quick-growing radish is a rewarding plant for children's gardens. One idea is to sow a line of radish seed to mark a row of slower germinating seeds.

Radishes

Cheerful variety

Radish colours range from the familiar red and white to pink, purple and black at one extreme and to yellow and green at the other. With their white flesh and colourful skins, this easy-to-grow vegetable makes a cheerful addition to your salad bowl. If your local market does not carry enough varieties, check a garden catalogue for the rarer types.

234

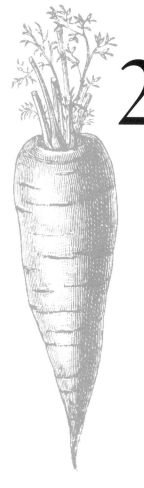

Cooked radishes

The quick-growing radish is typically eaten fresh, but if your crop out-runs you, and the roots become too large and a bit woody, you can boil them as you would turnips. Even very spicy radishes turn sweet and mild under the influence of heat.

235

Carefree crop

Radishes are a truly carefree crop. Possibly the only mistake you can make is to let the soil dry out, for then the tops bolt almost immediately and the roots turn woody.

236

Radish leaves

For a special, highly nutritious treat, sow radish seeds somewhat more densely than normal over a prepared bed. No need wait for the radish roots to form; pick the 1-in/2-cm-high leaves for a salad garnish or even, if you've sown enough, a complete salad. Have no fear—the radishes will produce a second crop of leaves and a healthy root in no time.

237

Since beans do not transplant well and, at any rate, are such quick growers, there is little point in starting them in pots. In an extremely cold and wet year, however, it may be worth a try with a few plants.

Beans

238

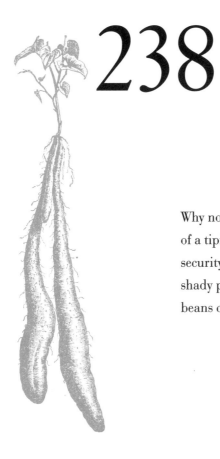

Beanpole tipi

Why not set your beanpoles in the form of a tipi tied at the top? It increases the security of the poles and will provide a shady play area for your children as the beans climb up the poles.

239

Don't touch when wet

Bean leaves are sensitive to being touched when wet. Contact disturbs the surface of the leaves and opens the way for disease. Therefore, tie and tend pole beans only after the morning dew has dried.

240

Tomatoes need a great deal of water, especially as they begin to blossom and set fruit. Before and after this point, over-watering encourages leaf growth rather than fruiting.

Tomatoes

241

Cutworms

To prevent cutworms from biting through the tender stems of young tomatoes and other vegetables and flowers, place a 4-in/10-cm nail halfway into the earth immediately beside the stem. Cutworms will be discouraged from reaching around the cold metallic nail and will leave your plants alone.

242

Deadly nightshade

Tomatoes are related to the deadly nightshade family. The fruit is safe to eat, in both its green and ripe stages, but do wash your hands carefully after working with the plants. The pungent odour imparted by the leaves lets you know if you have washed well enough!

243

Indoor ripening

If frost threatens before your tomato crop has ripened, no problem. Harvest all the healthy ones, red or green, large or small, and wrap each carefully in a bit of newspaper. Place them in a single layer on a shelf in a dark, cool cellar, and check them every week to sort out any that might have begun to go foul. Within several weeks, you will have your harvest of red, ripe tomatoes, no matter what the weather is doing outside.

244

Green tomatoes

Green tomatoes are excellent pickled. Heat them in a vinegar and water solution and seal well in clean jars. A few pearl onions make a nice addition.

245

Natural support

Odd as it sounds, the potato plant makes an excellent natural support for low- to medium-sized tomato plants. Set each young tomato about 6 in/15 cm away from a growing potato, and save yourself the effort of staking your tomatoes.

246

No need to plant your seed potatoes deeply—a hole of 2–3 in/5–8 cm is enough. You must only "hill up" the growing plants to a height of 4–5 in/10–15 cm above the earth to ensure that the potatoes are developing in total darkness.

Potatoes

247

Potatoes in a barrel

If you have limited space, even only a balcony, try growing potatoes in a barrel of untreated wood. Layer compost and soil in the bottom, lay your seed potatoes on it, and cover with mulch. When green shoots appear, add more mulch. Water moderately, and by the end of the season you should have a barrel-full of potatoes.

248

Fall care

In early autumn, as the leaves of the potato plant begin dying back, encourage the roots to make a last spurt toward maturity by cutting off the stem at ground level. Two weeks later, remove the potatoes from the ground with a potato fork and store.

249

Potato blight

If potato blight, usually associated with wet conditions, is a concern in your region, try growing potatoes under black plastic sheeting, which will shed a good deal of the rain. You will find your mature potatoes directly under the plastic cover, almost obviating the need for the potato fork.

250

New potatoes

For the delicate new potatoes in the spring, so good in salads or boiled and served with a little fresh parsley and butter, plant an early variety and harvest just as the blossoms begin to open.

251

Green potatoes

A potato whose skin is green because the growing tuber was exposed to light is unappetising but not dangerous. On the other hand, a potato with a green layer UNDER the skin is unripe and, as a member of the deadly nightshade family, may cause real illness. Be sure potatoes are ripe before digging them, and cut away any remaining green or greenish areas before cooking.

252

Frost protection

Although potatoes are a cool-season vegetable, young potato plants are fairly sensitive to frost and must be covered with plastic sheeting or straw when night frost threatens. Remove the covering in the morning.

253

Sweet potatoes

No true potato, the sweet potato is a starchy African tuber, particularly rich in vitamin A and roughage. It is therefore worth the effort to grow them in a glasshouse or under plastic in a warm area of the garden. Not only are the tubers excellent when lightly boiled, but the leaves can be eaten as spinach.

254

Cucumbers

In wet areas, you can set up a trellis for cucumbers to climb, and thus keep them off the damp ground–the vines will bear a surprising amount of weight.

255

Salsify

If your salsify bolts in the early spring before you have harvested all the overwintering roots, you can still pick the young, half-opened blossoms for use in
salads. When peeled and sliced, the roots are particularly delicious served
in a white sauce.

256

To avoid the need for heavy thinning later, sow carrot seeds in mid-spring rather thinly in the row. There is no such thing as an unripe carrot—you can cull the roots, especially those of early varieties, when they are quite young for use in salads.

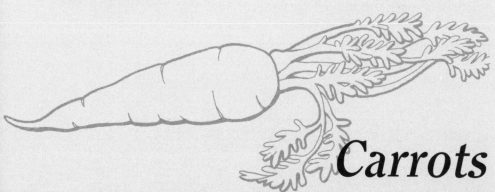

Carrots

257

Harvest and storage

Like many root vegetables, carrots may be stored in the ground in areas with a mild winter and harvested as needed—but these older roots are chiefly suitable only for the soup pot or stews. Otherwise, harvest the carrots 9 to 11 weeks after sowing, layer them in a sand-filled box, and keep in a cool place to be eaten through the winter.

258

Carrot flies

To ward off problems with the carrot fly, which appears only in spring, sow carrot seeds initially in a bed that can be draped with small-gauge netting once the fly makes its appearance. Afterwards, set the young plants in rows.

259

Proper soil

As a root vegetable, carrots require loose, sandy soil for best growth. They appreciate rich, humusy earth, and it is best to prepare the soil in the autumn for next season's growth. Avoid over-fertilising the roots while they are growing—they become hairy. Similarly, a fertiliser too rich in nitrogen encourages leafy top growth at the expense of the roots—not at all what the gardener has in mind!

260

Leafy tops

If you must thin your row of carrot seedlings—that is, before the roots have become edible—make sure to dispose of the leafy tops that you have picked away, for it is the odour of the dying foliage that attracts carrot flies to your garden.

261

Vitamin A

A fresh carrot contains more vitamin A than almost any other vegetable—the darker orange the better. Some of the round varieties of carrots are particularly rich in this nutrient.

262

Marking rows

Carrots germinate rather slowly. To mark
the rows and make it easier to keep the early
bed weed-free, sow quick-growing radish
seeds every few inches along the row of your
prospective carrots.

263

Roots and tubers

Root vegetables—including turnips and parsnips, beets and carrots, radishes and potatoes—provide garden fare throughout the year, either directly from the garden or from the cold cellar. All prefer loose soil for maximum root growth.

264

Beet seeds come in clumps. It is fairly useless to try to separate them and seems to interfere with germination. Sow the clusters about 1/2 in/1 cm deep and thin the seedlings ruthlessly when they appear, allowing only one plant per cluster to develop.

Beets

265

Germination aids

To accelerate germination of tough-walled beet seeds, soak them in warm water for half a day before planting. Another trick is to tap each cluster lightly with a hammer before sowing to crack the hard cases without destroying the seed material inside.

266

Eating beets

Beets are a versatile vegetable. You can cook young greens like spinach or add them fresh to milder salad greens; young beets (about 2 in/5 cm in diameter) may be culled and pickled; and older beets make an excellent winter vegetable when boiled with a little vinegar to preserve their colour.

267

Steady supply

Although beets prefer cool weather, keep a fresh supply on your table by planting at two- to three-week intervals throughout the summer, watering well, and harvesting before the tops bolt.

268

Winter storage

In mild areas, beets may be left in the ground for winter storage, especially if the soil is well drained. Cover the bed with a handbreadth layer of straw. In colder areas, pull the beets before a severe frost, twist off the leafy tops, and store in a cool, dry cellar.

269

Before you harvest

Beets like full sun; but before you harvest them, you can already begin setting out young seedlings of late cabbage and broccoli amid the beets. By the time the plants are big enough to cast shadows, your beet crop will be finished.

Mallows and squash

These quick-growing vegetables are easy to care for, as anyone who has found last-year's seeds sprouting out of a compost heap has discovered. In fact, squash vines offer an excellent way to hide a ripening compost heap—but of course this means you will not be able to turn the heap to speed up the com-posting process until the growing season is over.

Trellis training

In spite of the heaviness of their fruits, mallows and squash are, after all, vines and can be trained to grow on a sturdy trellis if garden space is short, or where wet conditions may lead to rot.

272

Kale

Kale is the gardener's friend in cold, wet climates. It can be harvested as needed through the autumn—and even dug out from under the snow for harvest in winter and early spring, as a new season's crop is being sown!

273

Brussels sprouts need deeply worked, humusy soil, which means preparing the bed with compost in late autumn. They also appreciate a light application of lime to the soil.

Brussels Sprouts

274

Planting conditions

Give Brussels sprouts plenty of growing room, about 2.5 ft/70–80 cm between plants. Good air circulation helps reduce fungal diseases, and sufficient spacing eases removal of snails and caterpillars from the plants.

275

Two crops

While Brussels sprouts are not truly cold hardy, they do benefit from cool spring weather. Sow the seeds twice for two crops—one in late summer and another in mid-autumn. In mild areas, sow again in the autumn for an early spring harvest.

Harvesting

Pluck Brussels sprouts before they show any sign of opening. It's all right to be selective—a few from this stalk, a few from that, leaving the smaller heads to continue growing. An added bonus: once all the sprouts have been picked, harvest the head of the plant and prepare it as you would cabbage.

277

Artichokes are members of the thistle family and require two years to produce a good head. Be sure to harvest your crop before the flower heads begin to open, however, or the results will be inedible.

Artichokes

278

Perennial artichokes

Renew or increase your artichoke harvest (perennial variety) by carefully cutting the side buds, along with a sliver of stem, and planting them 3–4 in/ 8–10 cm into the earth in the spring. Allow each plant a good 2.5 ft/80–90 cm radius for growth. After four or five years, the plants become "tired" and should be replaced.

279

Annual artichokes

The smaller, annual artichokes can
be raised from seed. Sow them in
late winter under glass, and set
them in the garden after all
danger of frost is well past. The
flower heads are considerably
smaller than those of the perennial
variety so do not wait too long to harvest
them, or you will only wind up with a thistle
flower rather than a vegetable.

280

Artichoke stalks

Like rhubarb or celery, the tender young stalks of the annual artichoke variety also make a tasty vegetable.

281

Jerusalem artichokes

The name is deceiving—Jerusalem artichokes are really a root vegetable and not at all related to the thistle-like true artichoke. Harvest the Jerusalem artichoke roots like potatoes in late summer, or store them right in the garden through the winter to harvest as desired. The summer harvest can be eaten raw in salads, or lightly boiled to soften.

282

The perennial Jerusalem artichokes are true garden giants, growing up to 10 ft/3 m tall. Plant them in a permanent location to the rear of the garden, and top them off at about 4–5 ft/1.5 m in late summer to prevent wind damage.

283

Soaking your cabbage seeds for half an hour in hot water before sowing will kill off any disease-causing fungi.

284

Rotating crops not only discourages disease build-up in the soil, but can also even out mineral deficiencies, since various plants have different nutritional requirements.

Crop Rotation

285

Nematode infestation

Nematode infestation of potatoes and tomatoes is relieved by moving these vegetables to another, nematode-free area of the garden and allowing the nematodes to die out in the old areas.

286

Combatting weeds

Crop rotation helps combat weed problems. A few years of potatoes, whose foliage tends to cast the soil beneath into rather heavy shade, will help clear the area of weeds and make it suitable for crops such as strawberries or onions, which are difficult to weed.

Legumes

The roots of legumes—plants of the pea and bean families—tend to fix nitrogen in the soil. After a year or two of legume cultivation, the plot will be ideally suited to the cultivation of nitrogen-hungry crops such as potatoes or members of the cabbage family.

Limitations

Rotation of vegetable crops is realistic only if it can be carried out over a relatively large area. If the garden plot is small, moving the crops a few feet away from their former beds will not cure deep-seated soil problems.

289

Nitrogen needs

Plants requiring small to moderate amounts of nitrogen (tomatoes, peppers, cucumbers and beans, for example) do well when planted to succeed the heavy nitrogen-feeders of the cabbage family (cabbage, broccoli, Brussels sprouts, kale and cauliflower).

290

Onions' cleansing effect

Members of the onion family have a cleansing effect on the soil, which makes them good successor crops for heavy-feeding summer crops such as tomatoes, peppers and cucumbers.

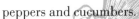

291

Pumpkin harvest

Late October means pumpkins. Harvest them before a severe frost and store in a cool place. Look up some good recipes for pumpkin soups, breads, tarts, and pickles to best take advantage of this vitamin-rich vegetable.

Eggplant

Eggplants—also known as aubergines—love warm weather but require a rather long growing period. This means they must be started under glass or on the windowsill in early spring and not set into the garden until the soil is warm. For an earlier harvest, try the Japanese varieties, whose fruit is ripe at a mere 3–4 in/8–9 cm in length.

293

True lilies

True lilies are members of the onion family and, as such, ideally suited for crop rotation or interplanting because of their ability to fend off pests and diseases. Try planting a border around your tomato or pepper plots.

Some plants simply do not "like" each other, and planting them in the same vicinity can lead to severe problems. Likewise, some combinations of plants are mutually beneficial.

Mixed Plantings

295

Dill improves taste

Not only does dill ward off garden pests, but many gardeners find that a planting of dill in the vicinity of peas, cabbage, lettuce, beets, and carrots improves their taste "au naturelle".

296

Strawberries and borage compliment each other nicely as garden neighbours. The herb will keep the berries free from plant lice and later provide a nice addition to your salad bowl.

297

A few nasturtiums planted among your peas and radishes will help keep plant lice at bay, and provide a colourful accent as well.

298

Cabbage protection

If your cabbage is bothered by ground flies and white flies, interplant your bed with lettuce against the former, and set out your young tomato plants nearby against the latter.

299

Carrots and leeks

Carrots and leeks make good neighbours. They foster each other's root growth, and the leeks will help fend off carrot flies as well.

300

Humble marigolds

Perhaps the gardener's truest friend is the humble marigold. They not only tend to keep harmful flying insects away from your vegetables, but their roots give off a substance distasteful to nematodes.

301

Radishes and other vegetables

Radishes thrive when interplanted amid numerous early- and mid-season vegetables including lettuce, kohlrabi, carrots, and beans.

302

Lettuce

Lettuce grows better when planted with carrots, and for a really quick-growing salad, try fertilising the ground with chicken manure.

303

Corn and lettuce

Corn and lettuce are good partners. The quickly maturing lettuce receives all the sun it needs before the corn has grown high enough to shade it too much. The corn, in turn, grows well into the summer after the lettuce has been harvested.

304

Thriving tomatoes

Tomatoes thrive when interplanted with parsley, carrots, and nasturtiums: Parsley improves their taste, carrots foster their growth, and nasturtiums help protect the tomatoes from plant lice.

305

Savoury and beans

Savoury not only appreciates the company of beans, it also helps keep the bean plants free of lice.

306

Root celery

Root celery appreciates beans and tomatoes as neighbours; they help the celery to grow more quickly.

307

One of the easiest ways to help fight insect damage is simpley to lure birds to your garden with a shallow, non-reflecting birdbath.

Pest Control

308

Onion flies

In gardens heavily bothered by onion flies, try planting onion sets rather than sowing seeds. The growing speed of the set onions will largely outpace any damage caused by the fly larvae.

309

Cabbage pests

Cabbage is not only plagued by white-flies, but also by diseases carried by weeds growing between the heads, especially common field mustard and shepherd's purse.

310

Rhubarb leaves

Not only do rhubarb leaves help trap snails, they also ward off pests from the cabbage family. Lay a carpet of leaves under growing cabbage plants, or steep rhubarb leaves in water and pour the brew on the plants and soil.

311

Snails

One good way to combat snails is to set shallow bowls or jar lids filled with beer around the garden in the evening. The snails are attracted to the beer and drown.

312

Gathering snails

Snails gather for cover in the morning under broad rhubarb leaves. Place a few of the leaves around your garden beds in the evening and collect the unwanted lodgers in the morning.

313

Mice

Dried oleander leaves, ground into a powder and sprinkled into mouse holes, drives the little rodents away.

314

Spraying against aphids

A weak solution of dish soap is an easy and effective way to combat aphids in the garden as well as on houseplants. Spray the upper and lower surfaces of the leaves of affected plants until wet (but not in the direct sun). The solution will not harm the plant. Repeat the applications every two to three days in dry periods until the newly hatching aphids have all disappeared.

315

Deterring plant lice

Cigarette and cigar ashes are an effective deterrent to plant lice. Simply scatter them on the soil beneath affected plants until the lice have disappeared. If the infestation is fairly light, use a light paintbrush to brush lice from rose stems onto a piece of paper, then dispose of them.

316

Garden grubs

To rid garden beds of grub larvae, sprinkle calcium on the soil in the autumn or winter and gently rake it in. Just take care to keep calcium-based compounds away from acid-loving plants like rhododendron, azalea, or rhubarb.

Rabbits

If rabbits trouble your garden, discourage them by enclosing the bed with a cord of twine soaked for several hours in kerosene. Protect young fruit trees from these pests by tying a layer of straw around the trunk, but be aware that soggy straw may cause tender bark to rot.

318

Climbing cats

To protect bird nests from marauding cats, tie a ring of long-necked 1.5- or 2-litre soft drink bottles, mouth up, about 6 ft/2 m high on the tree trunk, leaving no space between the bottles.

319

Cherry flies

Divert cherry flies from your cherry harvest. Just as cherries begin to ripen, festoon the branches with pieces of yellow plastic or foil coated with a sticky substance, or with contact paper.

320

Cabbage flies

A handful of wood ash sprinkled in the centre whorl of the young cabbage plant, just after cabbage flies appear, will protect the head from damage when the hungry larvae hatch.

321

Voles

Save your beautiful lawn from vole damage by soaking an old piece of cloth in kerosene—or, believe it or not, the juice from a tin of herrings. Place the cloth into one of the vole tunnels, and then seal it with a little earth.

322

Mouse scents

Mice avoid peppermint leaves, chilli pods, and cloves: Even a gardener who doesn't keep a cat can keep mice at bay without a mousetrap.

323

Fruit worms

Trap pesky fruit worm larvae in a layer of corrugated paper bound around the trunk of your fruit tree. Check the paper regularly, and when larva have collected, remove and destroy the paper.

324

Rats

Rats steer clear of guinea fowl. If you cannot keep hens, sprinkle valerian root where you see evidence of rat activity, stuff cloths soaked in kerosene into rat holes in the garden, and seal with earth. For a rat infestation, however, turn to a professional extermination firm for help, because rats can harbour dangerous diseases.

325

Cabbage caterpillars

To protect your cabbages from being eaten by caterpillars, mix several spoonfuls of wood ashes (an alkali) with the soil surrounding the young plants.

326

Scale insects are easily scraped from affected plants with a needle. Afterward, wash the leaves with a little soapy water.

327

In dry weather, a ring of sand strewn around your beds will ward off snails. With their soft underbellies, they much prefer smooth, wet soil.

328

Spider mites

To eliminate spider mites, wash affected leaves repeatedly with mild soapy water until the mites have completely disappeared.

329

Woolly aphids

Easily get rid of woolly aphids by washing affected plants several times with soapy water.

330

The hedgehog is a natural enemy of all sorts of garden pests, especially snails, and should be a welcome guest in anyone's garden. Tempt a hedgehog to make its home in your garden by setting out a saucer of milk for it in a sheltered place, unreachable by cats.

Welcome Wildlife

331

Toads

Toads are helpful against all kinds of pests.
Shade and a small pond or watery place will
make them feel at home in your garden.

Songbirds

Their melodies aside, songbirds' bottomless appetites for insects and other
garden pests make them welcome in any garden. Entice them into yours by
offering a few breeding boxes or even just some small, twiggy nesting materials.

332

333

Keeping chickens

If you keep chickens, pen them in the garden area in the winter and early spring. They will gladly rid your garden of harmful insects and larvae—and leave a little fertiliser in return.

334

Borrow a pig

For the richest possible garden soil, borrow a neighbour's pig to root around in the garden between the autumn and early spring.

Mowing with sheep

335

If you live in an area with sheep, you may be able to borrow several to mow your lawn, especially if you have a small orchard. But there is a price: Sheep will crop the grass very close, not the ideal for a prize-winning lawn surface.

336

Centipedes

Learn the difference between centipedes and millipedes, for centipedes are industrious consumers of snail eggs in your garden!

337

Share with the birds

Do not be upset at losing a few of your freshly sown seeds to the birds, for they will more than repay their debt later by ridding your garden of insects and small snails.

338

Frogs

Frogs are good warriors against pests large and small, from mosquitoes and plant lice to snails.

339

Water African violets indirectly by pouring water into the saucer, and avoid wetting their fuzzy leaves, which absorb the water and rot. Since the so-called African violet—not a true violet at all—is found in nature beneath tropical undergrowth, place yours in a warm room out of direct sunlight, and keep the soil moist but not wet. For a special treat, give these subtropical plants warm water to drink.

Houseplants

340

Subtropical plants

Poinsettia, African violets and orchids, all of which originally came from the subtropics, appreciate slightly warm water. In all cases, never let the soil dry out, but also avoid drenching their roots.

341

Yearly rhythm

Winter is a dormant period for both indoor and outdoor gardens. Taper down the watering and fertilisation of your houseplants in the autumn and pick up again in the spring, especially with the approach of the vernal equinox in late March. Houseplants are very sensitive to the increasing length of the natural day and require more nourishment.

342

Eliminate flea beetles from the soil of potted plants by inserting a safety match head down in the soil.

343

Soak new clay pots for 24 hours in water to leech out the chemicals used in the manufacturing process before planting anything in them..

344

Stained clay pots

To rid an old clay pot of ugly chemical stains, plug the drainage hole tightly with a cork or with waterproof tape, fill it with rocks and immerse it up to its rim in water. The water pressure will drive the stains back into the interior of the clay walls of the pot.

345

Clay pots and moisture

Ordinarily, clay pots are preferable to plastic or non-porous ceramic because the clay helps any excess water to evaporate. The drying effect of the clay also supports even root growth by discouraging roots from concentrating at the walls of the pot. The exception occurs in very hot locations, such as a sunny balcony or window, where impermeable pot walls help conserve precious moisture between waterings.

346

Good neighbours

For reasons scientists do not fully understand, houseplants tend to do better near other plants. But be careful; some plants—especially those with fleshy or hairy leaves—do not like to have their leaves in contact with those of other plants, preferring a close, but platonic, relationship.

347

Varying appetites

In both house and garden, some plants have greater appetites than others, needing more fertiliser during the growing season. Such plants are usually recognisable by their quick and/or heavy growth and include strawberries, tomatoes and corn in the garden; and geraniums on balconies or in the house.

348

Care of succulents

Even during periods of heavy growth, succulents need little fertiliser; in fact, an overdose can be fatal. Use a high-phosphorous fertiliser, and water the plant before fertilising to avoid damaging the delicate root hairs. Succulents are also more sensitive than most other plants to changes in temperature and need even more heat than cactuses—between 65-90 °F/20-32 °C.

349

Cactuses

Although we associate cactuses with the desert sun, the desert grows cool at night—and that is the way our cactuses like it! Especially in winter, cactuses prefer a half-dormant period, with temperatures between 40-50 °F/5-10 °C. In some areas, cactuses may therefore be kept outdoors, at least in pots that can be brought inside when a cold snap threatens.

350

Drying flowers

Tall, spiky flowers with small heads are the best for drying—simply cut them and hang them in loose bunches in a dry, well-aired room. To best preserve the colour and shape, however, select flowers just as they begin to open and gently lay them in a box whose bottom is covered with a mixture of 1 part borax and 3 parts cornmeal. Gently sift extra cornmeal over the flowerheads and allow to dry for a week.

351

Forced Bulbs

After forcing bulbs for winter enjoyment, set them aside for later planting in the garden. Do not try to force them a second year.

352

Unlike in the garden, bulbs for forcing should be set with their tips at the surface of the soil. Water well and remove them to a dark cellar for 8–12 weeks, depending on the variety.

Never let your forced bulbs dry out when they are in bloom. They will immediately wilt and lose their blossoms.

353

354

January

January, when the earth is either covered with snow or too wet to work, is a good time to put garden tools in order, clean your clay pots, and turn your compost heap if it hasn't frozen.

After a few hard frosts, your fruit trees should be dormant. January is a good month to do winter pruning--with the help of a good, illustrated garden book or a knowledgeable neighbour.

The Garden Year

355

February

No matter what the weather is doing outside, February is the month to begin sowing the earliest vegetables under glass (leeks and lettuce, for example).

To prevent the trunks of your fruit trees from splitting, paint them with lime. The gleaming white surface reflects the increasingly strong sun rays which can cause the sap channels to burst.

356

March

March is the right time to uncover roses and plant bushes and perennials. As the month begins, begin sowing crops of lettuce, beets, broccoli and radishes for a staggered harvest later in the year.

Also, give the growing buds of your fruit trees one last spray with garden oil to protect against the hatching eggs of harmful fruit pests.

357

April

April is the month to sow peas directly into the garden and to start cabbage and Brussels sprouts under glass. Spread well-rotted manure in your garden beds.

Rainy April is a good month to sow grass seed on a well prepared surface. If you wait longer, the germinating seeds might not survive a "drought" of several days of hot, direct sunlight.

358

May

In May, after all frost is over, you can consider sowing cucumber seeds and beans directly into the garden, but only if the weather promises to be consistently warm.

359

June

June is time to set out your late vegetables, such as cabbages, and sow kale for a late summer / autumn crop. You will need to begin watering your garden during hot dry periods.

360

July

July usually entails a serious battle against weeds.

Sow successive rows of bush beans for a regular harvest late in the summer. Allow your currants to hang on the bushes as late into July as possible to increase their sugar content. Make sure to have nets ready, though, to protect against hungry birds.

361

August

In the summer, many fruit trees produce so-called water sprouts–vertical, quick-growing "branches" that will never produce fruit. Prune these parasites in August, before the water sprouts have time to sap strength from the trees. Late August is a good time to set out your young strawberry plants in a bed vacated by one of your earlier crops.

September

Check your fruit and ornamental trees in September for dead wood, and remove it carefully. Dead branches may break away, tearing into the living substance of the tree.

While you can plant another row of kale in September, this is more a month for harvesting and for looking through spring garden catalogues to gather inspiration for next year!

363

October

When you're not busy canning, freezing or drying your harvest, October is a good time to plant flower bulbs for the spring.

364

November

November is time to clear out your summer garden beds and compost the remains—or burn what is diseased.

365

December

If the snow lies heavy and wet on your evergreens, gently brush it away with a broom to prevent the branches from breaking under the weight.